WINDSOR

ALLIGATORS AND CROCODILES

A TRUE BOOK®

by

Trudi Strain Trueit

Children's Press®
A Division of Scholastic Inc.

New York Toronto London Auckland Sydney
Mexico City New Delhi Hong Kong
Danbury, Connecticut

A Nile crocodile gently holding one of her young

Reading Consultant
Nanci R. Vargus, Ed.D.
*Assistant Professor
Literacy Education
University of Indianapolis
Indianapolis, IN*

Content Consultant
Joseph T. Collins
*Director, The Center for North
American Herpetology
Lawrence, KS*

Dedication:
*For Levi and Hanna, who make
the world sparkle*

*The photograph on the cover
shows a saltwater crocodile. The
photograph on the title page
shows an American alligator.*

Library of Congress Cataloging-in-Publication Data

Trueit, Trudi Strain.
    Alligators and crocodiles / by Trudi Strain Trueit.
        p. cm. – (A True book)
    Includes bibliographical references and index.
    ISBN 0-516-22653-3 (lib. bdg.)   0-516-29353-2 (pbk.)
    1. Crocodylidae—Juvenile literature. [1. Alligators. 2. Crocodiles.
3. Crocodilians.] I. Title. II. Series.
QL666.C925 T78 2003
597.98—dc21

                                                                    2002005877

Contents

A saltwater crocodile jumping straight up out of the water

A Crocodilian's World

Alligators and crocodiles have lived on Earth for more than 200 million years. Long ago, some were big enough to prey on their relatives, the dinosaurs. An ancient crocodile called *Sarcosuchus* (sark-oh-SOOK-us) was 40 feet (12 meters) long and weighed nearly 10 tons (9,072 kilograms).

Today's alligators and crocodiles aren't anywhere near that size. Even so, their bone-crushing jaws, armored skin, and powerful tails make them some of the most feared **predators** in the world. The saltwater crocodile can be 23 feet (7 m) long and can weigh up to 1 ton (907 kg). Alligators are usually less than 14 feet (4 m) long.

All alligators and crocodiles belong to a group of animals called crocodilians (crock-oh-DILL-yuns). Caimans (KAY-muns) are crocodilians

An American alligator in the southeastern United States (top) and caimans in Venezuela (bottom)

too. They are closely related to alligators. Caimans live in Central and South America.

7

A male gharial

The Indian gharial (GARE-
ee-uhl) is also a crocodilian. It
was named for the knot the
male gharial grows on the end

of its thin snout. The bump looks like an Indian pot called a "ghara." Gharials live in Nepal, Pakistan, India, and parts of southern Asia.

There are twenty-three different types, or species (SPEE-sees), of crocodilians: fourteen crocodiles, two alligators, six caimans, and one gharial.

Crocodilians used to be considered part of a group of animals known as reptiles.

Snakes and lizards are reptiles. Scientists have discovered, however, that crocodilians are actually more closely related to birds than to snakes and lizards.

Crocodiles can be found in the warm waters of Asia, Australia, Africa, South America, and the Caribbean. The American alligator makes its home in cooler rivers and wetlands throughout the southeastern United States.

The Chinese alligator lives in
a small area of eastern China.

Above and Below Water

The eyes, ears, and nose of a crocodilian are set high on its head. These features may be all that stick up out of the water as the animal swims near the surface. Above water, crocodilians have good senses.

When a crocodilian dives, skin flaps cover the ears. Muscles

A Nile crocodile swimming
near the water's surface

close off the nostrils. A flap on
the tongue seals the throat so
the animal can grab prey in its
jaws without swallowing water.
A clear eyelid slides over the
eye. Crocodilians cannot see
well underwater.

Crocodilians can stay underwater for up to two hours.

Crocodilians can stay below the water's surface for up to two hours. They are able to slow their heart rate down to just a few beats per minute so that they don't use up the oxygen in their lungs too quickly.

The thick skin of a crocodilian is covered with horny scales

The scales on a crocodilian's back (above) are thick and tough, like armor. The scales on a crocodilian's belly have no bone in them and are soft (right).

called scutes (skoots). Bony plates inside the scales on the animal's back act as armor. The belly scales are soft because they have no bone in them.

The top of a crocodilian's skin is dotted with sensory pits. These tiny spots **detect** vibrations in the water. The vibrations let the crocodilian know that prey may be nearby. Alligators have sensory pits only on their jaws. Crocodiles and gharials have them all over their bodies.

Crocodilians have webbed toes on their two hind, or back, feet. To swim, they fold all four legs against their

The skin around an alligator's mouth is dotted with sensory pits (top). Webbed hind toes (bottom) help a crocodilian swim.

When crocodilians swim, they move in an S motion (top). On land, they may crawl on their bellies or lift their bodies up and walk on all four legs (bottom).

bodies. They move in an S motion, sweeping their tails from side to side. Crocodilians can swim up to 6 miles (10 km) per hour. On land, they usually crawl slowly on their bellies. They may lift their bodies off the ground to waddle on all four legs.

When startled, some croco-dilians run or gallop toward the water. They may dash at speeds up to 11 miles (18 km) per hour—about as fast as a person can run. But you could probably outrun a crocodilian. They get tired quickly and can run fast for only about 60 feet (18 meters).

Croc or Gator?

An American
Alligator

Here are a few ways to tell the difference:

• Alligators tend to be dark gray or black.
Crocodiles are usually brown or greenish
in color.

- Alligators have short, U-shaped snouts, while crocodile noses are long and V-shaped.

- When an alligator shuts its jaws, you can't see its teeth. When a croc's mouth is closed, the largest teeth in the lower jaw are visible, jutting upward on the outside of its jaws.

An American Crocodile

Surprise Attack!

Gliding with only its nose, eyes, and ears visible on top of the water, a crocodilian waits for prey. A thirsty animal that steps into the river for a drink may mistake the croc for a floating log. When attacking, a crocodilian often uses its mouth to grab the snout of its victim, dragging it under the water and drowning it.

A Nile crocodile trying to grab a wildebeest

Only a few species, such as the Nile crocodile and the saltwater crocodile, will attack humans. In Africa, Nile crocodiles kill several hundred people every year.

The jaws of alligators and caimans snap shut with such power they can shatter turtle shells. Nile crocodiles are able to crush human bones. Yet the muscles that open a crocodilian's mouth are so weak that a person's firm grip can keep the animal's mouth closed.

A trained handler using his chin to hold an alligator's jaws shut

Crocodilians have a lot more teeth than humans do!

Most crocodilians have between sixty and eighty teeth. Gharials have more than one hundred teeth. Teeth are used for catching prey. Food is swallowed whole or torn into smaller pieces. If a tooth falls out, a new one will grow in. Over its lifetime, a crocodilian may lose and replace several thousand teeth.

Like reptiles, crocodilians are **ectothermic** (eck-tuh-THERM-ic). They rely on their **environment**, not on energy from food, for body heat. Crocodilians bask in the sun to get warm. They rest in the shade or slip into water to cool off.

Since they do not depend on energy from food for warmth, crocodilians don't need to eat often. Crocodiles have been known to go without a meal for more than a year. Young crocodilians eat insects, snails, and crabs.

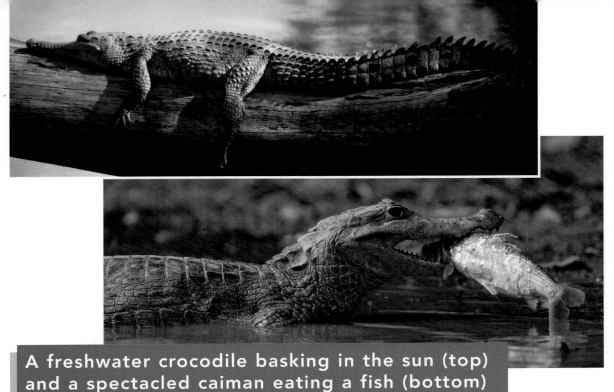

A freshwater crocodile basking in the sun (top) and a spectacled caiman eating a fish (bottom)

Adults eat fish, turtles, frogs, and rodents. Gharials, with their narrow jaws, can snatch only fish and insects. Larger crocodilians may eat zebras, deer, wilde-beests, and, rarely, humans.

Family Life

When courting, male and female crocodilians may rub snouts, swim in circles, and blow bubbles. They also "talk" to each other in growls, coughs, and purrs. American alligators bellow so loudly that they can be heard more than 600 feet (183 m) away. During mating

Alligators bellowing

season, you can hear their calls echoing across the wetlands.

Crocodilians mate in the water. They lay their hard-shelled eggs on land. To make a nest, alligators make mounds

An alligator
and its nest

of plants and twigs. Most crocodiles prefer to dig holes. Female crocodilians lay between ten and seventy eggs in a single **clutch**. The mother covers the nest well and guards it against predators. Monitor lizards, birds, opossums, and skunks often raid nests to eat the eggs.

In two to three months, the babies call out to their mother from inside their eggs. They make squeaking noises. While she digs up the nest to free them, they crack their shells using bumps on their snouts. This bump is called an egg tooth.

A Nile crocodile hatching from its egg

Newborn crocodilians are less than 10 inches (25 centimeters) long. The mother may pick up her hatchlings in her mouth and gently carry them to the water. Baby alligators remain with their

A baby Siamese crocodile basking on its mother's head

mothers for more than a year. They may bask on her head. This is the safest place to be. Herons, owls, snakes, fish, and other crocodilians eat hatchlings. Only one out of every hundred babies will survive to adulthood.

In a few years, a baby crocodilian will triple in length. Once it has grown to be 3 feet (1 m) long, the crocodilian has few predators. It then may live for many years. Alligators and caimans can live to be fifty years old. Larger crocodiles may live eighty years or more.

Saving Alligators and Crocodiles

Crocodilians play an important role on Earth. In the Florida Everglades, alligators use their strong tails and legs to dig deep holes in the marshlands. These "gator holes" fill with rainwater. They become ponds, some stretching more than 20 feet

A gator hole
in the Florida
Everglades

(6 m) wide. During the dry winter months when water is scarce, snakes, frogs, birds, deer, and many other animals depend on gator holes to survive. The American alligator is often called the Keeper of the Everglades.

Crocodilians were once plentiful on Earth. But overhunting by humans throughout the last two hundred years has wiped out millions of alligators and crocodiles. Some were killed

because people feared them. Others were hunted for their meat and skins. The skins were made into shoes, belts, and handbags.

Gharials have long been in danger of dying out.

By 1971, all twenty-three species of crocodilians were on their way to becoming **extinct**.

At that time, scientists figured that there were fewer than five hundred gharials left on Earth.

In the 1970s, the United States and other countries began to pass laws to protect crocodilians. **Conservationists** started special breeding programs to increase crocodilian populations. Crocodile farms were set up to meet the international demand for meat and skin.

Today, the Cuban (right), Philippine (middle), Siamese (bottom), and Orinoco (opposite) crocodiles are all endangered.

Today, two-thirds of the species have recovered. But crocodilians are not out of trouble. Pollution threatens many of their waterways. Human population growth is destroying their wetland **habitats**. Illegal hunting is also still a problem. Currently, the Indian gharial, black caiman, Chinese alligator, American crocodile, Philippine crocodile, Siamese crocodile, Cuban crocodile, and Orinoco crocodile remain **endangered**.

If these ancient animals are to have any hope of a future, humans must preserve and protect their place in the world today.

A Morelet's crocodile
in a tropical rain forest

To Find Out More

Here are some additional resources to help you learn more about alligators and crocodiles:

 **Books**

Markle, Sandra. **Outside and Inside Alligators.** Simon & Schuster, 1998.

Muñoz, William. **Waiting Alligators.** Lerner Publications, 1999.

Pope, Joyce. **Crocodile.** Raintree Steck-Vaughn, 2001.

Simon, Seymour. **Crocodiles and Alligators.** HarperCollins, 1999.

Thomas, Peggy. **Reptile Rescue.** Twenty-First Century Books, 2000.

Woodward, John. **Endangered! Crocodiles and Alligators.** Benchmark Books, 1999.

Organizations and Online Sites

Crocodilians Natural History & Conservation
http://www.crocodilian.com

At this website you can learn more about the size, habitat, and behaviors of each of the crocodilian species. Hear actual crocodilian growls, coughs, roars, and distress calls. See photos and videos of crocs swimming, galloping, and even jumping.

Everglades National Park
4000l State Road 9336
Homestead, FL 33034-6733
http://www.nps.gov/ever/ eco/gator.htm

Discover how gator holes shape the landscape and why they are so important to the animals of the Florida Everglades. You can also find helpful tips for keeping safe when you visit alligator habitats.

Crocodilian Specialist Group
Florida Museum of
Natural History
University of Florida
SW 34th Street and Hull Road
PO Box 112710
Gainesville FL 32611-2710
http://www.flmnh.ufl.edu/ natsci/herpetology/crocs.htm

This is a nonprofit organization of conservationists working to protect crocodilians and their habitats. The photo gallery has more than one hundred different crocodilians.

National Geographic Society
PO Box 98199
Washington, D.C. 20090-8199
http://www.national geographic.com

Go along as scientists search for fossils of ancient crocodilians such as *Sarcosuchus*. See how conservationists around the world are working to help endangered crocodilians.

Important Words

clutch group of eggs laid in a single nesting period

conservationists people who help preserve and protect wildlife

detect find, sense

ectothermic relying on the environment to raise and lower body temperature

endangered species that is in danger of dying out

environment surroundings of a living thing

extinct no longer existing

habitats environments in which an animal lives

predators animals that hunt other animals for food

Index

Meet the Author

Trudi Strain Trueit is an award-winning television news reporter and freelance journalist who has contributed stories to *ABC News*, *CBS News*, and *CNN*. Ms. Trueit has written many books for Scholastic on weather, nature, and wildlife. Her titles for the Franklin Watts Library series include *Clouds*, *Rain, Hail & Snow*, *The  Water Cycle*, and *Storm Chasers*. She is the author of three other True Books: *Snakes*, *Lizards*, and *Turtles*. Ms. Trueit has a B.A. in broadcast journalism. She makes her home in Everett, Washington, with her husband, Bill, a high-school computer teacher.